PARTNERSHIP
AMONG
BELIEVERS

Life Up Close and Personal

MR. MARTINIS BUTLER SR.

This book is dedicated to those that have been given another opportunity to_____.

PREFACE

This book is written to share answers to questions in a question and answer type of format. Many questions are asked, and individuals ponder them to come up with the right answers. This book does not say that the answers to the questions are all concrete guidelines that one should live by. One thing that this book acknowledges and would like to remind you of is that we are not perfect, and no two people think alike on everything. This could possibly allow God to reveal something totally different to you as it pertains to the questions and topics discussed and to further questions that may arise as you continue to read. Many things that are mentioned are things revealed to me through my life's journey, through testimonies, or even through other individuals' life experiences. Many will be able to relate to some things mentioned, and some will disagree. Keep in mind that the ideas may not line up with your way of doing things or your way of life, but there are biblical truths behind many of the things that are mentioned. Even Christians wonder and entertain puzzled thoughts about what goes on and what we involve ourselves with. One thing for sure is that if we allow the Holy Spirit to lead, guide, coach, reveal, and bring things back to our remembrance, and then we will be ok. Hopefully, after you read this book, you will not bottle up questions that you have, and you will be willing to help someone else who is going through the same questions. This is to formulate a "Partnership among Believers," despite our personal feelings.

Applying who, what, when, where and why's to a particular situation is something many wonder about, even when they involve your concerns for others. Have you ever asked yourself why certain things are the way they are as it pertains to life's situations? Why are we even concerned with the answers, when often times, we already know them? Sometimes it's good to share thoughts and ideas about particular topics, and key subjects. Why do we even allow the questions to formulate in our minds? Why does it even matter that we have answers to the "why" questions that arise? Many have come before us, and many will come after us who have yet to have the answers to their own "who," "what," "when," "where," and "why" questions. "Why" is probably one of the most powerful of the five W's? In any situation, all the W's are important, but to get into the mind of "who did it" and to find out what took place, where it happened, and when it took place, we still have to come back to the whole reason for why the other W's ever existed. It will always be in the minds of many individuals to ask why we even ask those intriguing questions.

CONTENTS

REASONS FOR PARTNERSHIP

A s partners, teammates, friends, family, acquaintances, associates, couples, lovers, and even soul mates, we are supposed to be accountable to one another. The Bible even tells us to pray for one another. We take those things lightly until something tragic happens. What if you have a best friend who means the world to you and you don't ever want to see that individual suffer. While this friend is at your house he decides that it is time for him to go home. As your friend packs his belongings in preparation to leave you notice that there is a turf war going on right in front of your house. You can hear the random gun-shots going off, and some stray shots even hit your front door. Would you stop your friend from leaving, or would you just tell him" See you tomorrow." and encourage him to leave? Of course you'd encourage your friend to stay until you knew it was safe to leave.

Many times, as friends and family, we say that we love one another and that we care about each other, but that's not truly where our hearts are. This is no different from what is expressed in (NAS) **Isaiah 29:13**: "Then the Lord said," 'because this people draw near with their words and honor Me with their lip service, but they remove their hearts far from Me, And their reverence for Me consists of tradition learned *by rote.'*" It sounds good when we express our love for one another verbally, but when we see individuals headed down the road of destruction, we don't express that same genuine love for them.

We need to be true partners for one another, especially within the household, as married couples. Men tend to draw up and project out their chests when confronted by peers or when afraid about a down-fall or issue involving the family that needs to be taken care of. They see things with tunnel vision, as if they are already doing all they can for their families, when in fact, the "doing" part is not the problem, it's more in the "listening" that the problem truly lies. As couples, we need to be able to set pride aside and be open to issues that we face constantly. The Bible tells us in (ASV) **Proverbs 16:18** that "pride goes before destruction and a haughty spirit before stumbling". So we need not be ashamed or set up walls to avoid hearing what others may be willing to share with us to help us grow as a better couple and to strengthen us as Christians.

We should be like Aaron and Hur during Moses's struggle. Moses encountered a time where as much as he loved the Lord and was a follower, he needed strength. Moses was in the middle of a battle and was required to hold his hands up throughout this whole ordeal, but fatigue was setting in. This was really no different from Christian journey that we are on daily, where we get tired and feel as if we can't go on anymore. Moses was unable to hold his hands up, and if they fell, then the Amalekites would certainly win the battle. However, Aaron and Hur stepped forth and held up the hands of Moses until the battle was won. Often, when we are helping others out, we are so wrapped up in getting the glory or being seen for what we are doing that we miss the chance to truly witness and get a word through that could possibly impact lives and drastically make a difference. Moses was a God-fearing man whom God called to lead his people. In our situations, as in his, it is people like Hur who are considered the true pillars of a friendship, marriage, or any type of relationship that needs tending to. It's those individuals in the background who rise to the occasion, not for the glitz and glamour, but to see lives changed and souls saved. Its individuals like Hur who dare to stand out just to see a war won for the good of everyone involved.

Let's continue to inject Bible scriptures where they are needed in order to be there for one another and also to exhort one another in such a way that God gets all the glory. The Bible admonishes us in (AMP) **Hebrews 10:25,** "Not forsaking or neglecting to assemble together [as believers], as is the habit of some people, but admonishing (warning, urging, and encouraging) one another, and all the more faithfully as you see the day approaching." The time of God's return is too close for us not to be there for one another and assembling together to build one another up. We must come together to hold each other up, especially if we have issues that need to be taken care of. You should already either be speaking over someone's life in a positive light or be receiving counsel from someone. Many ask, "Well, do we need to come to church to hear a word from the Lord? What's wrong with listening to the word on TV or buying CDs?" Those methods of getting a word are totally fine, but God wants us to assemble together. Encouraging one another builds us up to be proficient and well equipped. Coming together also allows us to use our gifts together to glorify God. There's really no substitute.

It's no different from working out. You're an individual who loves to work out and go to the gym, but for a month you are unable to go to the gym. What do you do? Sure, you do what you can with supplements and pills as substitutes until you can get back into the gym to get in a real work-out. It's similar when dealing with the Christian faith; supplements and pills are like Cd's and biblical pamphlets. They are great just to keep you afloat, but you really wouldn't continue just using those without being around other Christians for strength and encouragement. Just as iron sharpens iron, Christians need to be around other Christians and a leader just so he or she can get stronger and have a Shepherd to speak into their life. If you were to take pills day in and day out, those pills and supplements would be useless without exercise. You take supplements to get big and strong, which are ok, but when you are looking for a change, you have to go the extra mile. There's no substitute for being with your Christian family, and that's why it is so important to attend church and attend Bible study. That is not to say that if you do not go to church or be assembled with Christians, you are going to hell, but there is strength in numbers, which adds another reason. This is especially important during trying times such as the ones that we are facing now.

Understanding different roles in the household as it pertains to marriage should be understood. Even society has expectations as to who should take responsibility for certain actions that take place within the home. Should society truly have a say in what goes on, and what is God's take on it? In many cases in marriage, men are entrusted and held responsible for much decision making that takes place. The basic standards never change, but the guidelines seem as if God and society expect a little more of men, their roles, and how different things are approached. Men tell their wives that they will love them and cherish them no matter what, during the good, and the bad, in sickness, and in health. As Christian husbands, we are to be priests, providers, and protectors of our homes and especially of our spouses. So why is it that we seem to be confused as to our titles in the household? We remember that children should be obedient and that wives should be submissive to their husbands, but we seem to forget that we have jobs as the leaders and the heads of households, not to dominate but to make wise, godly decisions that is pleasing unto God. Society fights with us about whose role it is to do certain things as it pertains to providing for and taking care of the home.

What happens if the husband and wife are both in good health but the family loses their home and is forced to live out on the streets? Honestly, who will be considered by outsiders not to have pulled their weight, thus allowing this type of incident to take place? About 90 percent of the time, the finger will be pointed toward the male figure of the home, simply because of the image that society has placed on the man of the house. Questions may arise as to why didn't he make sure he took care of his family., he's supposed to be the head of the household, isn't he?, or so he supposedly says. Obviously, something went wrong, possibly there was poor management of finances, someone wasn't paying bills, or perhaps there was some other internal issue the family may have had. Very rarely will society look upon the female and assume it stemmed because she didn't cook a hot meal for him, or assume she didn't massage his feet when he wanted it, or believe she didn't keep the sex hot in the marriage to ensure that he worked hard to keep a roof over their heads. These are things you think of but refuse to say, for whatever reason. We must remain cognizant of the different things we do and how we think when things go wrong. We must be careful of assumptions in our thought processes, for we know that our families often play intricate roles in the lives of believers.

CATERPILLAR
TRANSFORMATION

W e could be compared to caterpillars in reference to our life cycles on earth. We were born into a world full of sin. The sin in our lives came from the predestined mistake that Adam and Eve committed. We were never intended to stay the same way that we entered the world, physically or spiritually.

When we are born, we are babies who are ignorant to many things that are around us. As the years pass, we are expected to grow and become wiser. Like caterpillars, we should grow into our natural forms. There must be a process or transformation that takes place on the inside as well as the outside. During a caterpillar's' first stage, it begins on the ground and crawls around the earth along with other caterpillars.

Then it must be in a position and a place in its life where it is ready to begin a new cycle of life. In time, that allows the caterpillar to transition into its metamorphosis stage. In the end, the process occurs during which the caterpillar becomes a beautiful butterfly., It will then soar across the earth and be able to see those other caterpillar's that have made the transformation as well. If we compare humans to these butterflies, we can only envision those other caterpillars, or human beings, still crawling around on the ground and still slithering in what we will call their sin.

The Bible tells us in (NIV) **Romans 12:2,** "Do not conform to the pattern of this world, but be transformed by the renewing of your mind. Then you will be able to test and approve what God's will is His good, pleasing, and perfect will." God never intended for us to stay the same way we were when we were born, just as he did not create the caterpillar to stay as a caterpillar forever. Once an individual comes to the Lord confessing, believing, and receiving, there should be a change, and that person should want to soar above that old lifestyle just as the caterpillar has done. Once this process happens, we as Christians (butterflies) should never allow ourselves to feel inferior to anyone else or make anyone else feel inferior to us. There has just been a change on the inside that allows an outer change to be displayed before others.

We are never better than those who have not yet made the commitment to undergo the Christian transformation, but we should be in a better place because we now have direct access to God through Jesus. Just like butterflies after being changed, we must continue to fly back to encourage, evangelize, and be witnesses of the goodness of God that has allowed Christians to realize the truth. We must also keep in mind as well that it's good to get a reality check and never forget where God has brought his people from. We must never allow those sinners (the remaining caterpillars) to draw believers back into a lifestyle that is not pleasing unto God. As we go on in our daily lives, we should lend a helping hand to help those out in the world that aren't Christians see the truth, especially those that are interested in the faith. This journey will be rough because not everyone will accept Christians for who we are and what we are trying to pursue. It is still our job to help believers as well as non-believers, whether they want to receive it or not. Never allow someone you love to suffer or take on an issue alone if you can prevent it, unless it's a trial that God wants that individual to go through alone. At least be there for moral support, especially if you've just come through a similar predicament.

SEEKING
APPROVAL

W hy do we allow others to dictate who we are as individuals? Many of us feel as if we do not have the approval of others, especially those individuals who seem to have made a name for themselves by doing something different. We tend either cower down or make ourselves feel inadequate. When was it made ok and who made it ok for those not in the church to mandate what should be going on in the church and how it should go on? Many times it's the individuals we look up to or perhaps even want to pattern ourselves after who are making those ungodly suggestions. There are people in the world who envy other individuals lost within the world and who are seeking the approval of average individuals for answers.

There are many people who are not relaxed and confident in their own skin. Why don't believers dare to be different? Why do they really feel that others should be the authoritative figure that approves what they do and the decisions that they make? Many celebrities dare to be different and are corrupting the lives of many individuals by what they say and especially by their actions. There are times when those individuals are unaware of how their decisions affect lives across the world. Then there are many times when they are aware of their actions, but they refuse to change to make positive impacts and lead lifestyles that are suitable so that others can really be blessed.

Why would you pattern your life after anyone who is not willing to set a positive example or try to be a good role model so that others can benefit? It's mind-boggling that people glamorize stupidity, fool-ishness, and drama but refuse to shed light on positive behaviors or on individuals who truly make a lasting positive impact on society. Is it truly pressure, to step out of your comfort zone to allow others to see the God in you? Why is it that an individual who works a regular nine-to-five job, takes care of their family, and is an avid, law-abiding citizen doing something to enhance his community's well-being just receives a handshake? Whereas a celebrity who has made millions of dollars by acting or singing, doesn't take care of any of their children, but decides to donate hundreds of thousands of dollars just for attention receive so much acknowledgement? Often times, the donation are not sincere but are used as a tax write-off, yet that individual receives ten times the rec-ognition. Is it that society is truly blown away by an individual's status or what they feel makes that person relevant? It's truly mind-boggling to know that this type of behavior is well accepted among us.

We as a nation proclaim that we would like to see change, we would like more positive things being done within our communities, and would do all that was within our power to ensure that this happens, but we re-fuse to make such changes individually. Why are we sitting around not making a difference, but become one of the first to criticize what things evolve into when times get hard? No doubt, many of us have problems, but not many of us have conjured up good solutions for those problems. That's why we must maintain that partnership, that relationship among believers to help each other press toward the mark.

IMPACTING
LIVES

Why do individuals who are in a position to impact lives and make a difference feel as if it would diminish their social status or destroy their public personas by opening up about their struggles and heartaches? Many times, it's those celebrities and famous individuals who are making themselves out to be superhuman. Hard times and obstacles are eye-openers to some individuals, prompting them to press on to achieve goals that they have set out to accomplish. Christians consider such trials and tribulations to be tests or obstacles that God has allowed them to go through so that they may come out as the victors, rather than as victims. I strongly believe that sharing your struggles, heartaches, and pain allows others to see the positive outcomes. This encourages others to be stronger in their walks with God, especially if they are going through similar issues. A problem that may take you five years to overcome may take someone else only five minutes to overcome, just from you sharing your testimony. Testimonies' can truly be soothing to the soul and may also be refreshing to someone else's.

Have you ever wondered why people claim to have your best interests at heart but always seem to be the ones that are constantly taking away from you? Do you ever wonder why, when you have the opportunity to confront them about an issue, you just can't seem to express yourself as you would like? Have you ever told yourself that you would have done something, and would still do so, if only you were to get another opportunity, simply because the first time wasn't exactly the right time? What seems to be the hold-up? What seems to be the problem? Why all the excuses? We are people who seem to be secure in being comfortable in the positions that we are in.

Many individuals refuse to step out of their comfort zones for fear that they might expose weaknesses that they have. Such exposure often makes us cower away from the truth and sometimes discourages us from succeeding. Individuals who confront their fears are the people who are the most comfortable with themselves. If you keep things bottled up, this often results in pain for yourself, and that type of pain could very well cause you either to hurt someone or hurt yourself. The pain that's inflicted is very seldom physical pain, but it is emotional pain. Emotional pain tends to tear you apart slowly, but it usually has a lasting effect on you.

We should be open with people about our feelings and innermost thoughts. People sometimes don't know that you're hurting unless you express your feelings and concerns. Many times, we assume that others know what we are feeling and why we do what we do. Have you ever wondered why you built up the courage to confront someone, but as the outcome panned out, the situation didn't unfold as you believed it should? Sure you were open, sure you told the truth, you even put your heart into it and even shed a few tears in the process, but somehow, things just didn't work out in your favor. Why was that? In some cases, you may never know why. It may take years before you receive an answer. You may never receive an answer, but one thing you can rest assured about is that you got it out in a way in which you felt comfortable. Although the end result wasn't what you expected, you shouldn't have to feel guilty because you did what you had to do. Things are not always going to go in your favor, and there will be good days and bad days. The Bible tells us in (NIV) **Ecclesiastes 1:9** that "What has been will be again, what has been done will be done again; there is nothing new under the sun." God sees all, and he knows all, so what you're going through now or in the future has already happened before you have experienced it.

Having a relationship with God should result in a separation from the world if one is genuinely committed. It could also result in a separation from God if we do not stay focused on a strong, steady commitment to him. For example, what if you are new to a neighborhood and you are eager to make friends, so you go on to meet a couple of individuals? Later on, you might try to get in good, just to be friends with them. The friends you meet have everything you want, and you simply admire them for many of the things that they have. You would like to be in their situation, but you are aware that you do not have the means to afford the lifestyle that is being displayed in front of you. Typically, as with any new friends, you wouldn't want to burn any bridges or get on their bad sides. You already have in your mind that you're willing to do everything it takes to stay liked because after all, those individuals are giving you those things you so longed for. You're also puzzled because things are coming so easily to you, and your newfound friends assure you that you are in good hands. Anything that you are in need of you should bring to their attention; after all, that's what friends are for.

Now months have passed, and you start to feel as if you can do just as much on your own and without the assistance from your friends. Now you forget the friends that you once had and forget the promises you made to these friends that you'd never leave or turn your back on them. (Tough times will never last forever, but tough people will.)Years go by, and your wealth starts to run low, and you start to feel as if you are an outcast among your friends. You go back to them, asking for their support despite the snobbish attitude that you've displayed toward them, and to your amazement, they accept you back with open arms.

That's no different from when you finally accept Christ as your personal Savior. He is not only a friend, but he is everything that you can ever imagine in a person, and more. You can't be too impatient and refuse to wait on God. When you refuse to wait, you are opening up doors for mishap and possibly allowing the devil to turn your life into shambles. Just as with your friends, if you decide to return back to God, by asking for his forgiveness, he will be open to receive you. Remember, God is not a God of a second or third chance; he is the God of another chance. We should never limit God to the favors that he can give to us and has given to us.

COMPARISON OF LIFE-STYLES

We often wonder when we look at the hand that God has dealt, why we don't feel as if we have what we deserve in comparison to others. Why do we compare our success to that of individuals who seem as though they have it all? We know that we should not be comparing ourselves to others, and we will be the first to admit that it's wrong, but somehow, we have these *buts about* why we do it. Do we really want to go through what the next person went through in order to get what he or she has? Do we really want all the glamour and glitz that these celebrities are being portrayed to have? Are we really willing to give up all that we have for someone else's lifestyle?

We say that we don't want everything that the next person has, but we want to pick and choose what we receive and how we should use it.

God has a plan for everyone, but he will not force our hands to make us do anything. Even though God has the power to make us do anything but wouldn't, but that doesn't stop Him from making us wish that we had done it. Many times, those things come from Him placing boundaries or making it difficult for us to achieve those things that we wanted. We become so confused to the point where we just can't seem to make our minds up. Sure, when it's beneficial for us, we would love to dictate our futures and the paths we take to be successful, but when God reveals to us what He wants us to do and where He wants us to go, we simply place God at a standstill until we are ready to react. Sorry, it doesn't work that way. We are constantly asking, but we are not constantly doing.

Why do we feel the need to try to negotiate with God for what we want? We want to come to God when it's feasible for us, but when things don't line up; we want to hit the pause button until we really need Him again. Then we hit the resume button. We know about all the things that are going on in society. God indeed is a God of multiple opportunities, especially when He knows that our hearts are right. We should not limit God or estimate how many times He will come through for us. We should continue to be obedient and allow Him to order our steps.

Many people feel that life is not fair. We ask God the questions, "Why me," "Why this," and "Why now," when faced with trying times. The questions should be, "Why not me," "Why not this," and "Why not now?" Sure, you may not have the big house, the fancy cars, or the nice clothes, but why not focus on the positive things that you do have? Look at the life that you still have as opposed to a life that someone else doesn't have. Look at your good health as opposed to that of someone who is on life support. Look at the means you have to be able to use and enjoy your five senses as opposed to the means that someone else doesn't have to use his or her senses, for whatever reason. The Bible tells us in (NIV) **1 Thessalonians 5:18** that we should "give thanks in all circumstances; for this is God's will for you in Christ Jesus." That means that in the good and in the bad situations, you should still be grateful. Now, you may be thinking, why in the world would I give thanks during the bad times? Have you ever thought about being content with what you have? What about those who are less fortunate than you at that very moment? What about the lesson that you could teach someone simply by staying positive in a rough situation, which could allow someone else to better handle his or her situation? Often-times, more things are caught than taught, meaning that in the society that we live in, people are observant. They are more likely to watch an example and live by it than to hear someone just talk about a situation and not even live by what he or she speaks.

TECHNOLOGY
DISTRACTIONS

W e are living in a world where technology has taken over. We are substituting it for everything that we do and use just for the sake of how efficient technology is. We have overcome many leaps and bounds to get to where we are today. If it had not been for technology and new inventions that people have discovered, we would not be able to accomplish many of the things that would be required of us today. God has blessed us with minds that are able to develop many of the things that we use today. I don't believe God has opened doors for us and then expect us not to use them at our leisure. We should not be afraid to step out on faith to follow our dreams and be creative. We should not be intimidated to learn and speak our minds. (KJV) **2 Timothy 1:7** encourages us by saying, "For God hath not given us the spirit of fear; but of power, and of love, and of a sound mind." We should be bold and persistent in all we do, especially if it could benefit a good cause. We see that modern technology has made it possible to commute more efficiently, communicate effectively, and work more productively. In the midst of all the transitioning to modern gadgets and an updated means of working, we have lost our way. We have gotten away from what has made us who we are. We are giving up what means the most to us simply because of technology.

Marriages are being broken up because of all the technology that is out today. Social media are raising our Children and have started to corrupt many families. From Facebook, to MySpace and now Twitter, individuals are forgetting what the word "privacy" means. It's more like marrying the world. We post so many pictures of our lives and daily events that before we can truly enjoy our events, others on these social media sites are enjoying them for us. There's no denying that many families are losing the direct connection with their loved ones. Long before cell phones, families actually spent quality time together. Dinners were times where you could bond together. Before cell phones, family members actually took advantage of the chance to be open and to speak about their day. Without cell phones, members of families were able to be themselves and be understood.

With social media and the ability to text and tweet, individuals are forgetting what it was like to communicate face-to-face. This has taken us away from being truthful and sincere. Years ago individuals used to run to one another's houses to give them information. The ability to write a sincere letter with meaningful words was another way to go. Asking someone to go on a date meant something for the individual being asked. The other party would invest a lot of time in preparing what he or she wanted to say and would take time to go the extra mile to make him or herself look presentable for approval. In this day and age, people text to ask others out. We show emotions by sending facial icons via phone messages. I believe so many relationships don't work because all through the dating phase of the relationship, the individuals have been texting and sending e-mail messages. So when the people are married, things fall apart. They truly haven't invested that time to truly get to know one another for who they are. Facebook, MySpace, and Twitter open up passage-ways to other individuals to creep in on our relationships, especially if we are not strong in the relationships. We've gotten to the point where we are hiding account information from one another. We start making secret accounts, hiding our computers and phones, being secretive about passwords, and perhaps even sneaking off to indulge in sinful doings. We should start being mindful of the time we invest into these social media sites and how much time we spend on our personal gadgets.

Are you allowing your phone, computer, or maybe the television to draw you away from a closer relationship with God? If so, you are truly allowing that "hellaphone" and "hellavision" and all these modern pieces of equipment to take up more time than God would allow.(NLT) **Exodus 34:14** tells us that "you must worship no other gods, for the LORD, whose very name is Jealous, is a God who is jealous about his relationship with you." "We should not let minor distractions keep us away from what God wants to do in the lives of his children.

BE CAREFUL WHAT YOU ASK FOR

O ften, we hear people say things that they really shouldn't be saying, and sometimes, people say things that aren't true, yet through our experience with the people, we sort of wish were true. How silly is that? Many times, we are those people, and we catch ourselves in the midst of saying things that eventually through days, weeks, or even years, we wish we had never even spoken. How ironic is that? Why don't we just let things be? For example, you may have children of your own, while your friends are married and don't have any children and refuse to have children. Why is it that people ask ignorant things of friends whom they know? In this example, for instance, you might ask questions like, when are you going to have

Children?" You might pressure your friends and even back them into a corner with questions that should make anyone feel guilty. People also say things with crazy motives. They could be questions such as, "Why aren't you guys having children yet, "followed by comments like" You are not getting any younger", or other questions like "Why are you guys being so selfish", or, "Did you know the Bible says to be fruitful and multiply?" Or you could even remind the couple of what your children means to you and the excitement they bring to your life.

These may be people who have expressed on multiple occasions that they have no time for children, perhaps because children are career stoppers, perhaps because they are not comfortable with children yet, or maybe because they just enjoy being a couple without any children. You pressure them, knowing they are not remotely child friendly. What if this couple has a child a few years later and the child is at the age where he or she is really a problem when it comes to being obedient? The child seems to be a bit much for the couple, and from your experience with children, you can tell that this is a little more than what this couple can bear. You see the two of them on several times on different occasions with their child, and you know there's something you should say, but you would rather go home and gossip behind their backs about how rude that couple's child is. First of all, what type of friend are you? If there should be anyone helping out, it should be you. You showed an interest in them when they were childless, so why wouldn't you lend your so called expertise now when they are in need of your advice? That's how many of the individuals in society behave. Whatever makes a good story they allow to spread like wildfire. Keep in mind that if you seem to recognize or bring up the notion of having a problem, it would be in your own best interests to come up with a solution.

I just don't know why people say they love God and praise him with their mouth but then curse and say all sorts of nasty, disrespectful things out of that same mouth.(ESV) **James 3:11** asks," Does a spring pour forth from the same opening both fresh and salt water ?" Would you go pick up trash from a Dumpster with your hands and then grab a slice of cake with those same hands and eat it? Really, the concept is no different. In this day and age, we are individuals who are concerned about what others think of us. I think if we spent more time trying to encourage our peers to be positive and took a stand for something and did not just fall for any old thing, perhaps we could make a difference among the people who love us the most. Let's stop contributing to many of the old habits that we see today. Let's be careful of what we say. We need to be more aware of the people that we surround ourselves with, simply to avoid those toxic speakings to enter into our ears.

DECISION POWER STRUGGLE

Why is it so difficult for people to be submissive to their leaders? Why is it a constant struggle for individuals to realize that they are not always going to be in the position of being a leader?

In today's society, people have the knowhow to lead but in many cases everyone is not called to do so. Many are even capable and equipped but the timing may not be right for them at that present time. Some people when ask to take charge or to voice their opinions in public, they seem to cower down or run away from the opportunity to do so. What makes you so qualified to make statements or come up with your own opinions on how to run the country, lead group functions on your job, suggest different ways to run functions, or say what you will and won't do when you are not asked to give your input? Many people are backseat drivers or behind the scenes delegators, but they do not have the nerve to be bold and firm and to make decisions that would benefit the masses. The army constantly tells it junior leaders that when they are in charge, they should be in charge and not wait until someone else is coming so that they can become limelight soldiers. The individuals who often have the biggest effects when it comes to accomplishing a mission are those who are doing the work and are not all about getting face time. In other words, those are the individuals who walk the walk and not just talk the talk. Everyone will have his or her day.

What will you do when given the opportunity? What will you do to make the difference? Who will you be when called upon? Will you be that individual who has so much to say but who refuses to make a true difference, or will you be that individual who will step up to the challenge when called upon? Will you be that individual who is willing to put forth the energy to ensure that he or she supports the next person's vision and is a good follower?

Have you ever wondered why it's so confusing to make a decision that could potentially alter the course of your life if made poorly? We often time find ourselves being luke warm to certain issues. We sometimes find excuses to play the happy medium. By not wanting to go too much to the right and not too far left being in the middle seems to make majority of the people happy and doesn't seem to ruffle too many feathers in the process. Who are we really fooling? Who are we really impressing by our decisions? Other religions and cultures are so compassionate about who they serve that many are willing to die for their beliefs', but if someone were to approach you from behind and say, ""Denounce Jesus and I will spare your life," would you do it? Would you be that individual who tries to bargain his or her way out and then asks for forgiveness later? We know that the United States is truly built on Christian values, and the world knows this to be true, but why are we so comfortable in giving credit elsewhere? Why is this ok with Christians? Why aren't enough Christians making a big stink to try to bring more souls to Christ?

In a time of crisis, the country was willing to come together to have a national prayer day. In our courtroom's, people raise their right hands and swear to tell the truth on the Bible, and not on any other religious book. The president swears/affirms on the Bible when he takes office, and no one rejects that. The Bible has been the number one selling book in the world for years, so why do people not recognize this to be the one and only true source that has the truth in it? Think of another book besides the Bible that has prophecies from years ago that are still coming to pass today. Exactly, there is none! Who are we to question God as to why certain things happen? Is it ok to ask, or isn't it? We know that God allows things to happen for a reason. The Bible tells us in (CEB) **Mathew 5:45,** "so that you will be acting as children of your Father who is in heaven. He makes the sun rise on both the evil and the good and sends rain on both the righteous and the unrighteous." Individuals who are living a righteous life aren't the only ones God is blessing with prosperous lives and good fortune.

Becoming a Christian should be the biggest event in your life above your wedding, childbirth, getting any degree, or even losing your virginity. Why do friends and family find it the hardest to believe that you have chosen to take a stand for Christ? There may be decisions that you may have to make that will result in you having to dismiss family members because of the stance that you have vowed to commit to. Remember, these are the people who would know you the best. These are the people who have seen you in the lowest of the lows and the highest of the highs.

SETTLING AND REVEALING A GLIDE PATH

I f a book foretold something years before it happened, and it all came true years later, why wouldn't you believe it? This has happened time after time on multiple occasions without anyone having a clue that these events would take place, so why aren't more people made believers? We are living in a time where we will just settle for a lie before the truth; we would prefer someone to whisper sweet nothings in our ears rather than for something to happen that would change our lives for the better. (NLT) **2 Timothy 4:3** tells us, "For a time is coming when people will no longer listen to sound and wholesome teaching. They will follow their own desires and will look for teachers who will tell them whatever their itching ears want to hear." We are so offended because the truth is revealed to us in a harsh way. Does that really matter? Should we really care? We need to place our feelings aside and focus on the changes that this truth could bring about, not only in our own lives but in the lives of others. If someone shows you how you can live forever, have the desires of your heart, enjoy life, and find true happiness, why wouldn't you seek after this? Why should the answer to that question be delayed? Jesus has given us a strip map and has given us the tools to reach that accomplishment.

The Bible is our basic instruction book before leaving earth. If everything is already outlined for us, why aren't people motivated to find out what it has to reveal? It was not written as a promise that you will never suffer or have pain or problems. The Bible will definitely guide you in directions that will help you to avoid some issues that may come your way. Being focused on the Bible while listening to the Holy Spirit will teach, coach, and mentor you through obstacles. Who in their right mind, when given all the right answers to life's test, would refuse them, especially when those answers are given to them to use?

The Bible reveals so much more truth for today than any other book written in its time. Things are constantly revealed to us and people ignore the signs. Many feel as if those signs are coincidences, and others feel they are nothing more than sheer luck. This attitude would be understood if it occurred with just one or two things, but time and time again, the Bible hits it right on the nail with everything that it reveals. We should use the Bible as our Global Positioning Service and allow the Holy Spirit to be our voice navigator. If we hide God's word in our hearts and continue to meditate on it, both night and day, it will help us maneuver a whole lot more smoothly during life's intersections and road-blocks. The devil constantly places these road blocks in our paths and even starts construction on the journey, trying to bring us to a stop in our tracks.

How would you feel if you were swimming in a pool without a lifeguard, especially if you couldn't even swim? In (NIV) **Psalm 121:3, the** psalmist say, "He will not let your foot slip He who watches over you will not slumber." God will watch our feet and prevent us from slipping from his will." The lifeguard sits at a high place to observe anyone in trouble. God also sits in a high place to observe our every move. The lifeguard blows a whistle when danger is at hand; God blows his Holy Ghost whistle to warn us and prevent us from getting into trouble. Just as lifeguards know how to respond to trouble, God knows exactly what to do as well. You have people who are willing to swim without a lifeguard present, just as they sneak into the pool when it's closed. Christians have a lifeguard who is always on duty, no matter what time or day it is. Even when we get into a situation, a lifeguard knows how to revive us, just as God does when it's necessary. When we go out too far and start drowning in the world's problems and start to sink in sin, we must be willing and call on the name of Jesus. Jesus will come to our rescue. Ask for forgiveness, and he will be faithful to bring us back up afloat. When individuals constantly approach you saying, "Man, why are you always talking about how blessed we are and talking that Jesus talk, trying to act all different?" you should tell them that it's the truth, and what else is there that is more important than that? Don't you think we have enough people telling lies, acting ignorant, and being foolish?

RESPECT, AND WHO DO I TRUST?

Whatever happened to respect for the church? There used to be a time when an individual could be driving by a church, playing loud and obnoxious music, and that person had the decency and respect to turn the music down or turn it off. The person would never pull into a church yard being disrespectful. Whatever happened to a time when alcoholics wouldn't dare crack bottles open near the church and they definitely would not throw bottles on or near a church lawn? What happened to the time when a smoker would be so ashamed even to smoke around the church? Those who felt that they couldn't help but to smoke would literally hide around the building, out of plain view, just to get one or two puffs in. They knew exactly that what they were doing wasn't pleasing not only to God but definitely on the church premises. We have gotten so complacent in what we do. It's not so much the people who don't know but it's the people who do know, who refuse to say anything about it. Years ago, it was unheard of for many of these types of events to happen. People feared God and didn't want to be on God's bad side. People were so cautious about what they said that even when individuals thought they had excuses, they were at least aware of what they were doing. Even if they were drunk or high, they knew that in the mere mentioning of God' or Jesus's names, they should conduct themselves in an appropriate manner.

How is it that we live in a society where the cops get more respect than what God is entitled to? Whatever happened to people recognizing the pastor, bishop, apostle, or a man of God who served the role of speaking over the lives of people on Gods behalf? Why is it that anybody can call the pastor on his cell phone and just ramble on for hours as if they are best friends? Whatever happened to doing things in a decent and orderly manner, according to the Bible? We have the elders and the ministers of the church to assist in those matters. The problem is that you have so many leaders trying to either straddle the fence or not being committed to doing the work of God whole heartedly. This is why you have those bishops and pastors of particular flocks feeling the need to take on so many responsibilities all on their own. There are so many people serving in positions of leadership, yet many individuals do not want to make an honest commitment either to those positions or even to God. Many lost souls are out there waiting for a word or for someone to set the example.

Many faithful church attenders are upset by things that they see in the church. The leaders in the church should be aware that many times, things are going to get rough and that people are going to bash them just for the sake of them being Christians. They should continue to stand strong and firm in what they believe. Many times, all it takes is that new

Christian or churchgoer to see an individual in a leader's position make a mistake that contradicts the word, and this could very well result in that individual becoming confused about what to do. Already such new believers are looking for Jesus in the leader, and they could very well be thrown off track because of anything that they see or don't quite understand from the church. We know that we are not perfect and that they should not be looking at us but at the Jesus in us, but sometimes people who are new to the faith may not understand this fact, at their early stages in the Christian walk with God. That's why we as Christians have to be just that much more cognizant of what we do because we are already living our lives under a microscope before the world. Leaders in positions of authority should also be cognizant of how they counsel and what they say to others. Many individuals who come to church for direction or for Godly counseling feel as if they can't even trust the individuals in the church. Many fear that the leaders may gossip and tell others their business. Leaders need to seek God for direction and also be led by the Holy Spirit.

WHO DETERMINES LIFE?

I s there truly a real meaning to the term, a "cursed blessing?" Does it have to be both? What if you had a child by someone who raped you when you had been saving yourself for that one true, special love? You were really going to wait on God to send that individual who you had been praying, asking, and fasting for. Now you're stuck between the decision of whether to have an abortion or keep the baby. You are living a righteous Christian life and don't believe in killing. So who determines the future for the child? This is a big tug-of-war in which many people today fight. I believe it depends on the situation. When I say "depends," it's not just about either killing a baby or allowing it to live. It depends on the current condition of whoever is carrying the baby and depends on whether this is the best thing for the child, as it pertains to health issues. If the risk of death does not exist, then I strongly believe all children should have the opportunity to live. The individuals who disagree should put themselves in that situation.

What if you were the baby and the main topic of an abortion discussion was about you? Would you want people gambling over whether you should live or not? The Bible tells us that in all things we should give thanks, so why wouldn't the life of a child be a good thing to give thanks for? In no means is rape acceptable under any circumstance and the victim is the one who has actually witnessed or have lived the horrific event. Many individuals would have mixed emotions as to what they should do with the child. Sure, you may have those females who support abortion because they feel that if a woman is not ready, then the choice should be hers. You may also have those females that believe whatever the issue or circumstance is life is a precious gift that should be cherished. We live in a world where we have choices, and the choices we make should not cost someone else their life if is negligence to the individual. If a female is having sex loosely, unprotected, irresponsibly, not married, or even prostituting and comes up pregnant how should the world view this type of conduct? We as a people live in a world where adoption is a great way to go, and there are couples who can't wait to have children but are unable to. These are the small things that people should take into consideration before making choices for the future.

TAKING A STAND

Taking a stand means laying it all out on the line, being passionate, and bold on whatever you are trying to relay. Preachers should have that same mentality for delivering the pure unadulterated word despite the backlash of the world or fear of losing members in the church. Sometimes being straight forward when preaching could possibly disturb the way people live their life. Some preachers feel the need to preach on redemption, while others focus on informing people that the wages of sin is death. There's preachers that believe preaching should be inviting and shine the light on the good news of God. The Bible is known to be called the Good News. Often times a word from The Lord convicts people all by itself. Sure, pastors should preach a word to save souls and inform people that Jesus loves you, especially after having a troubled week. What should be preached to individuals that are having an amazing week living in sin? What type of message should be delivered to those individuals? Shouldn't they be warned about the lifestyle that they live? Of course a word of conviction sometimes is what people need to allow them to recognize the destructive path that they may be headed towards.

Is there an easy way to express the hard truth even if the hard truth causes you to stand alone where many would believe that you should think otherwise? Say, you have a good friend who is a homosexual and in a relationship. Your child asks you in front of the couple why is it that two men are married. Of course, your answer on a personal, quiet note was that they have love for one another and that was what they wanted to do. The follow-up question from your child would be, "Can I do that if I want?" What should you say, and how should you give the child that answer? You're a Christian, so you want to honor the word of the Bible. You believe that the Bible is specific about relationships being between men and women. Would you stand firm, or would you water the facts down, as society would have you do, just to avoid any confrontation? Would you prefer to stand and face the scrutiny of the world as opposed to standing and receiving a place for all eternity?

The Bible tells a story about a man named Lot, who had two virgin daughters. The story becomes interesting, and different people may receive a different understanding as the story unfolds. Some individuals will get a different message as it applies to their lives or as the Holy Spirit reveals what is needed to be understood. Now, two male angels came to Lot's home and were threatened with gang-rape. What makes this story so intriguing is the way in which Lot tried to appease the attackers. At this point, God had decided to destroy the city of Sodom. A pair of angels had arrived in Sodom to rescue Lot (nephew of Abraham) and his family. As the angels waited in Lot's house, the men from the city gathered outside his home. The men were banging and yelling for the two angels to come outside. If you have an imagination, especially from what is being displayed on television today, about how your typical rapist may act and how aggressive he might be, then you can assume that this was an emotional event for Lot's family. So Lot went outside and closed the door behind him and attempted to reason with the crowd by saying, "Look, I have two virgin daughters. Let me bring them out to you, and you can do with them as you wish, but please, leave these men alone, for they are my guests and are under my protection" (NLT) **Genesis 19:4–8.**

Yes, you imagined correctly. Lot offered his two virgin daughters to the assemblage of Sodomites in an attempt to avert the aggressive attack on the angels. I think the plea to "do with them as you wish" is particularly interesting, given who he's talking to. Unfortunately, (or fortunately, depending on whose side you're on), this wasn't enough to satiate the lustful appetites of the horny Sodomites. God came to the rescue, however, striking the attackers blind and giving Lot, his family, and the angels the chance to escape. The two insights that I took from the story were that rape is no joking matter and that it is prohibited. Obviously, there is a reason, if a man is willing to give up his two virgin daughters to protect two male angels whom he does not know, to allow some out of control Sodomite strangers to have their way with them. His daughters could be potentially killed in the process, which says a lot about how much it is despised for same-sex relations and rape to be allowed.

FINANCIAL GAINS

Do you call the financial gain from gambling, playing scratch offs, and even hitting the lottery something that you would categorize as a financial blessing? Do you really feel that it's OK to do these things, especially if you are a Christian? Well, I guess some would feel that it should be ok, simply because they give the church a percentage. So God couldn't possibly be mad. Do you believe He should be? You even go as far as giving a tenth, which the Bible requires from you. Well, I bet you should really feel as though you have done something when you give money to the less fortunate. We ask, why or how could God be upset with me? Oh, I know, let's compare ourselves with other rich individuals and see who has done the most with what he or she has. Clearly, those so called unselfish individuals are going to feel as if they have cases to dispute before God. By no means am I to say what is gambling and what is not gambling, but what I will say is that if by any chance what you are doing brings true conviction to you, perhaps you should take heed and harden not your heart.

We have heard others say time and time again, "Don't judge me," or, "Only God can judge me." True indeed; we should not judge whether you're a Christian or not. We do not want to falsely accuse someone of something, especially when we are jumping to conclusions. The Bible tells us in (NIV) **Mathew 7:1,** "Do not judge, or you too will be judged."

CHOOSING NAMES

Why aren't names as important as they once were, and why don't they hold great meaning, as they once did long ago? Just to inherit a meaningful name from a father was prestigious and carried a title of self-worth. People would give their child a name that would set them apart from the so-called average child. Nowadays, children are being named some of the most outlandish names known to humanity. It's as if families are content with catchy names as opposed to names that carry a sense of value. Names are so important because they allow a window of opportunity before judgment is cast upon you and before people meet you. Often, names define who you are or what you stand for, especially nicknames. Why would you give yourself a nickname that lowers yourself worth? Why not depict a name that allows you to be noticed in a positive way or that even tells a story about you? Back in the day, names were announced as royalty in some places. People wanted names that would allow others to know they were honorable or that their families meant something.

In most cases, last names told a story about family history. They helped define the who's who of last names. Would you name your child Rapist Johnson, Serial killer Jenkins, Masked murderer Grant, throat slicer Hernandez, DUI White, or even Deadbeat Myers? Those names may sound hideous, but they also seem even worse as you are addressing someone. We need to get back to where we can be proud to say, "I am pleased to be affiliated with that particular name or individual." It's the small things that we need to take into account. It's often decisions such as this that we take for granted that could potentially alter the course of an individual's life. As children grow up to become adults or perhaps venture out to find themselves, parents should consider setting their children up for success. In society, stereotypes are still being used among us every day. Children and adults are becoming outcaste because of what they call themselves or what others perceive them to be. We should not be potentially setting our children up for disaster before their careers begin. Many times, it's the small things that could potentially make us or break us.

TAKING ADVANTAGE
OF FAMILY

F inance is a topic that often seems to rattle cages when mentioned. It's something that can go either way. It could go in your favor, but many times it involves someone wanting a handout as opposed to someone lending a hand up. Who gives friends and family multiple breaks after he or she has been taken advantage of? When is enough, enough? Should you count the favors that you do? Some would feel that if you have to keep count of the favors, then you either didn't mean your favor from the heart or you must have been doing it for notoriety. Some may also feel as if family members can take advantage of you for the sake of love and just because they are family. What a golden opportunity that could be. Many people take advantage of opportunities to manipulate family into doing things for them. Families often feel backed into corners because of what other family members may say if they don't render assistance. I believe that you have the right to offer or refuse any help that you choose.

Even though we are Christians we should always be willing to help those in need. People may be in need of something and if we could be a blessing we should be open to doing so. We are blessed so we can be a blessing to others. Being a blessing and being taken advantage of are two different things. You should allow the Holy Spirit to reveal to you which issues that you should plunge feet first into to be a blessing and which ones that you should just pray over and allow God to move in his own way and at his own time. We should always ask for direction from God before we do anything. Ask yourself what would Jesus do in a situation such as this and allow the Holy Spirit to guide your thoughts. Be mindful as well that if you ask what would Jesus do, you would have to know him to come to that conclusion.

MISUNDERSTOOD

O ften times a people say, "I don't regret anything because the mistakes I've made have made me stronger, have made me a better person, or have made me the individual that I am today." Could that be true? Should that be the case, especially if the person knew that the path he or she was headed down was a hellacious path? As Polonius in Hamlet states, "To thine own self be true." "Many people are homeless because of poor decisions made behind stupidity, families have broken up over quarrels, jobs have been denied, and lives have been lost as well as lives being taken because of poor choices. Think for a moment. Sure, you've learned from mistakes and could tell the stories, but the most intelligent individuals are able to learn from what other people's mistakes have been and not by trying the same thing themselves. There are times when people may want to get the facts for themselves and may want to experience things on their own, but why would anyone need to suffer or put themself or someone else at risk, knowing the consequences he or she may face?

Is it possible that God could be saying two totally opposite things to two different people about the same incident? For example, there could be two different men who have witnessed a horrific tragedy such as a death in the family. One man is so involved in what his family does or says that this totally distracts him from hearing God. This man truly loves God, but his family is a priority to him, and he has started concentrating on family more than taking his problems to God to handle. Mind you, God wants you to love your family, but at the same time, God is a jealous God as well. So God reveals to him that he needs to shy away from his family for a while and seek God's face simply by praying and fasting in order to really see what God wants to tell him. His doing this will prevent his family from becoming a distraction to him. Now, the next man is so in love with God that he is seeking God every chance he gets, and when the doors of the church open up, he is right there, praying and worshipping. God loves when we make him number one in our lives, but he doesn't want us to neglect spending time with our wife to the point where the word "divorce" is starting to become the hot topic of discussion in the home. This man knows that God is not the author of confusion, but it seems that he is confused and being tugged in two different directions. By no means is he even thinking that he needs to make a choice as to whom he will obey and follow. Who will it be that is revealed to him, his wife or God? It's revealed to him that he needs to focus a little more on his wife's needs and pray that God will allow his relationship to be stronger than it has been. Often God gives us an answer and draws out which direction we should go or where we should find our answers but many times, we want to place God on pause when it's convenient for us, and whenever we are ready, we want to hit the resume button in hopes that God will just pick up where he left off.

Why do people feel that because certain phrases have been around for a while and have been believed, they hold some type of value? They often try to validate the phrases by saying that the Bible says this or the Bible says that, without the sayings even being in the book. Many times it's because people aren't reading and studying the Bible like they should to find out what it says for them. The Bible tells us in (NIV) **2 Timothy 2:15,** "Do your best to present yourself to God as one approved, a worker who does not need to be ashamed and who correctly handles the word of truth." It's irritating because we say things so much that we start to believe them, including phrases such as, "God helps those who help themself." Now, how could this be? What if you are unable to assist yourself? Does this take you out of the running to receive a blessing? Of course not, there were individuals in the Bible who were assisted by others, those who interceded just to save someone's life, or those individuals who physically assisted in ensuring that individuals made it to Jesus. How about, "If you take one step, God will take two?" Seriously? How about, "What doesn't kill you will only make you stronger," in regard to going through trials that God allows to come your way? Individuals need to be careful of the things they say, especially when they mislead people about what's in the Bible.

WHERE DO YOU STAND?

Who are you, a leader or a follower? Granted, not everyone can lead all the time and some people are not leaders at all. We all can be followers, and when we follow, we must be sure that we are following the right individuals and for the right reasons. We may not know everything, so that's where, many believe instincts or one's conscience comes in to play. "Many people look at the conscience as though there are two angels fighting one another to persuade an individual to make choices". Then you have Christians who believe in what is called the Holy Spirit. The Holy Spirit is a person, the third person of the Trinity: Father, Son, and Holy Spirit. He is a person in every way just as God the Father and Jesus the Son. Many people also believe that the Holy Spirit brings things back to their remembrance and acts as a guide, a teacher, and a leader.

To explain the Holy Spirit from a personal stand point the Holy Spirit could be seen as a jumper cable as it pertains to a car battery analogy. For Christians that need to get that connection to hear from God as well as be fired up or rejuvenated they seek the help of the Holy Spirit. If a car battery is dead it would need to receive a jumpstart from another source that already has power. That power on the other end would be another vehicle that has a battery with a stronger battery life. In this case the dead battery would be the Christian and the vehicle with the stronger battery in which the alternate power source would be coming from would be God. For us to be able to start up we would need to be connected, and what would connect us would be jumper cables, in other words the Holy Spirit. Once the jumper cables are connected to both batteries, then and only then will that dead battery generate enough power to be able to provide the necessary power that the car needed to have to allow that vehicle to make it to its next destination.

Many times we choose not to listen, and that's what gets us into trouble. Would you be willing to be a leader and take a stand for Christ if you were called to do so? Would the pressure from peers get the best of you? Many individuals crack under pressure and just follow along with whatever sounds good for the moment. People often say, "If you don't stand for something, then you'll fall for anything." In most cases, that is a true statement. If you won't be strong enough emotionally to express and demand things, then it's going to be a struggle for you to be a leader. No one wants to follow someone who is unsure and doesn't have a plan for where he or she is going. You have to be persuasive in your dealings. Being prepared at all times discourages your foes, and your competitors. Many times, being equipped frustrates the devil when you hide God's word in your heart and know when to use it while being attacked.

Society wants us to believe that the majority rules, as it pertains to decision making or when votes are involved. What if someone tells you that the God you serve or believe in is not at all what he claims to be? How would you respond? What if those same individuals go so far as to say he doesn't even exist, how would that alter the course of your thinking? You may not know how to respond if you're not equipped and strong enough to take it. For starters, we as Christians should be able to tell others about the goodness of what God has done in our lives. You may start to question, what if God's not real. How could this even be a thought after he has proven himself time and time again in so many instances? So you ponder the thought, is there a God, and how do you know that the one you are serving is the correct one, and what validates him being real? How can this notion be explained? The answer is simple; it's all in the *Bible*. The Bible reveals distinct truths that no one should second guess or begin to decode. There is not another book in this world that remotely comes close to the truths that it reveals.

What if you were told that there's no heaven and there's no hell? If there isn't a heaven or hell, do you get to live irresponsibly? Can you act out of control or even convert back to your old, sinful ways? If you're doubtful, why not just live according to the Bible? If there's no lake of fire, then you have nothing to fear or worry about, but if there is a hell then you just bought yourself a one-way ticket to eternal damnation. In (NIV) **Psalm 34:8, the psalmist** says, "Taste and see that the Lord is good; blessed is the one who takes refuge in him." Why not prepare yourself for the worst and expect the best, instead of not doing what God has for you? No one can say he or she is willing to spend all eternity in torment and totally be content with that idea. Can you afford to take that chance? I don't think anyone can. It's a hot risk that no one could or would enjoy for any length of time let alone all eternity.

The truth often hurts, and there are going to be times where you have to face the truth. The truth about life, friends, family and what to endure and things that we may not have been warned about growing up that we would face in the world. Life is a constant struggle, and you're going to endure heartaches and pain. It was never promised to us that life's journey would be easy because if the journey and everything else in life were going to be easy, then the whole world would be taking that route. As you see by the current state of the world today, not everything is planned and unfolds in a way that we would expect. Just believing that you're in good hands and will be taken care of by God and you are only basing this off of the life style that you are living. Many people know who God is simply because of what their parents or friends have told them. Many people have seen or heard of many of the miracles that God has performed. Basically, many people may say they know God, but truth be told, they only know of him and don't truly know him personally. Just knowing about him and his wondrous works does nothing for your soul. To truly know him is to have a relationship with him. It has to be more than just memories about God and living off of other peoples testimony's, you need to experience this life changing experience and take on the opportunity to know God for yourself.

To know Christ, you have to be willing to spend time with him and find out his likes and dislikes. It's no different from going on a date when you really want to surprise your date with something special for his or her birthday. You think of ways to communicate, spend time researching, studying, and exploring ways to see what your date is about. One date won't allow you to know all that you need to know to take the relationship respectfully to the next level. The more time invested, the more you know and get to learn about your date. If you're really in love with this person, you think about him or her all the time and it seems as if you can never get enough of that individual. Well, it's just the same when you really need to form that relationship with Christ. You have to spend time with him and get into his word to find out his likes and dislikes and the plan that he has for you. The Bible tells us in (NIV) **Joshua 1:8** to "keep this Book of the Law always on your lips; meditate on it day and night, so that you may be careful to do everything written in it. Then you will be prosperous and successful." No relationship works without communication. Christ wants us to make a vow and keep it, and he also trusts that we will serve him with all that we have.

Why are we so hesitant to hear from God? Obviously we are because we don't pray and seek God as much as we should. Everything now is as quick as instant grits or microwave popcorn. No one wants to fast and pray until God changes or intervenes in a situation. We are quick to make judgment calls because we don't see the speed of God according to our personal radar speed gun. Back in the day, men of God such as Moses and John the Baptist could call people together and have as many people as in a town or village wanting to come out just to hear a word from the Lord. These days, it seems as though we are so busy that if God doesn't move, we want to force God's hand to move in hopes that we will get the results we want. Sorry, it doesn't work that way.

What happened to getting people together to have prayer meetings? Whatever happened to going out door to door praying for the sick? Whatever happened to stepping out in faith, trusting, that if you pray, God will have an answer for you if you will just only believe? What happened to people coming together even closer than the neighborhood crime watch? It's just upsetting that we cry because God doesn't answer prayers on our time or doesn't honor our plans, but we are the first ones to start looking to God when all else fails or we have no other way to turn. In years past, there were individuals who were willing to bring their children to the church to instill good morals and allow them to invest time in receiving good, Godly counseling. There are just not enough couples who are praying together and coming in on one accord to get a word or a prayer through. On the other hand, you have some individuals who will tell you that they are praying for you but have yet to go into their prayer closets for themself. Have anyone ever approached you who were less fortunate, homeless, in need of a job, or who just didn't have anything at all? Have you ever ignored such a person when you've been too busy to lend a hand?

One of the most common things Christians utter is, "Before I do something or lend out money, I have to pray about the situation." Now, why do you need to send up a prayer for something that you know you can be a blessing at that moment? There are many things that people need right away, but they do not get the help they need because of individuals trying to be too saved or trying to act holier-than-thou. There are some things that you know you don't need to go all out to pray and fast for. If you see a need, why not allow the Holy Spirit to guide you? For example if someone hasn't ate in four days, and you have a bag full of food or you have a pocket full of money, are you seriously going to leave that individual there in need? Of course, you probably would, since we do such things all the time without even letting it bother us. There are so many people who do these things but refuse to see the hypocrisy in what they do.

WHO IS MARRIAGE DESIGNED FOR?

When God designed and made everything perfect, he saw that Adam needed a companion, someone he could be with, grow with, share a life with, as well as be fruitful and multiply with. God knew that the only way for this to take place, allowing what he had set in place to unfold just as he wanted, was to give Adam a woman. He would design her for Adam to enjoy and to bring all that God had thought of into existence. David wrote in the book of **(NIV) Psalms 139:14** "I will give thanks to You, for I am fearfully and wonderfully made; Wonderful are Your works, and my soul knows it very well." To take it a step further, in (KJV) **Genesis 1:27**, it states,

"So God created man in his *own* image, in the image of God created he him; male and female created he them.

We know God to be perfect, with no imperfections. This is true even if we are distracted or we disagree with someone's appearance, a minor birth defect, with special needs or even a major defect such as being born disabled.

God created us so we should know that he knows the beginning and the end. Why would we question God about how we look or how someone else looks? God designs and allows individuals to cross paths for a reason, so if someone is disabled or is born differently, we should still consider it all joy and give thanks in all things, despite how we feel. The main point here is to shine the light on why God created Adam, and why in addition to that did He give Adam a female companion. Many people in society feel that men and women are intended to be with whoever makes them feel good. If that is the case, then why didn't God arrange for the world to unfold in a different way? Why didn't God create Adam and Eve and another man and another woman? That way, Adam could truly have had the choice of being with a man or a woman. We believe that Adam was a smart individual and God trusted him obviously because He entrusted Adam to name all the animals in the garden. If Adam wanted to see a different image, he could have very well had asked for a replacement for Eve once she appeared. If God wanted him to be with another man, then he would have given Adam the man in the beginning with no option. Many people know about the Old Testament prohibition against homosexuality. (NIV) *Lev 18:22 "Do not lie with a man as one lies with a woman; that is detestable"*

God designed a female body with different functions and with a different figure to endure all that He has set forth for women to do. Obviously, God is so intelligent and great that He knew that the only way to reproduce was to have a man and women to come together to reproduce. As it pertains to humans there is no other way that it is possible to have a child. God gives us the power and ability to make wise decisions about who we want to spend the rest of our life with and choose the love path that would best suit the individual. Absolutely, many do have that decision making ability. God allows us to choose and make decisions, but when we run into issues involving those things that God forbids us to do, then we should understand his decision to help us when we get into those situations.

If you're warned about doing a certain thing on your job, and it's against the job policy, and you intentionally do it anyway, knowing you might get fired, do you protest against it when you're caught? Do you tell the news that you knew you were wrong but intentionally did it anyway? Do you try to sue the employer, go to court, and plead guilty? Of course not! It's in your contract not to step outside the lines of what is required of you on the job. It's no different from the way that God has already established his laws (his do's and don'ts) in the Bible. When we disobey, how dare we try to reason with God about why we are doing what we are doing? The world often tries to make the Christians walk into a gray line. But the world's views do not decide what God has planned for a man and a woman. As Christians, we must be direct and straightforward about what a marriage is. We know marriage to be a sacred thing between a man and a woman, not between a man, his boys, and his wife, and not between a wife, her girlfriends, her husband, the parents and the children. Marriage is simply between the husband and the wife, and everything else is secondary. In (NIV) **Ephesians 5:25,** it says "Husbands, love your wives, just as Christ loved the church and gave himself up for her."

2010 Random House Kernerman Webster's College Dictionary defines a wife as a woman joined in marriage to a man and considered as his spouse. Synonyms often times used to define a wife are woman, spouse, lady, and female. The 2006-2013 Kernerman English Multilingual Dictionary defines a husband as "a man to whom a woman is married. Known synonyms for a husband that are often used in society today are words like hubby, spouse or married man. In no way did God allow two men to be in a relationship or two females to be in a relationship, let alone be married to one another. Society has altered the way things have been outlined in the Bible and allows people to call each other life partners, love couples, or even marriage companions. Not to be judgmental or to sound as if this type of behavior is a deal breaker to make friends, but this is not accepted among believers. Christians do not hate the individuals who live this type of lifestyle, but they should hate the sin that stems from this type of conduct and life style.

A great comparison is that this is similar to having a family member who is in an abusive relationship. The family members find out and confront the abuser, informing the person that this type of conduct is not accepted in the family. This is not to say that the family members hate the individual but just that they want the individual to know, as a part of their family, their views are that this type of behavior is unacceptable. Granted, no one person is the entire family as a whole but they are just an individual within the family who speaks on its behalf. As Christians, we are members of a family that believes that we should love the individual and hate the sin. We are just speaking and taking a stand on behalf God.

Christians are individuals who are supposed to set good examples because they are held to a different standard than nonbelievers. When we know better, we are supposed to do better. If the question is asked, "Is it OK for two men or two women to be in love and get married, "the only answer is, "No." In explaining it, we would call it living in lust rather than being married. It would not be of God, and God will not promote it or be a part of it in any way, shape, or form. If God was to honor this arrangement he would be a liar But the Bible says in (KJV) **Numbers 23:19,** "God is not a man that he should lie; neither the son of man that he should repent: hath he said, and shall he not do it? or hath he spoken, and shall he not make it good?"

People sometimes joke that before marriage, an individual should be able to check the man or woman out first. Potentially spouses should be treated like cars, where you have to test drive the product before you buy. To many people that could come off as rude and inconsiderate. What if all men thought like this about women before marriage? What if all women thought like this about men before marriage? What if your loved one were referred to as a car and was so called "test driven" by different drivers until the current owner was satisfied? How would you feel? A woman's heart should be so hidden in Christ that a man should have to seek Christ first to find her. The same goes for a man's heart as well. Then, if a man really seeks to find a woman worth it, he already knows where he needs to check. Many individuals wonder why their relationships do not look as promising as they would like. Women are at an all-time low in their self-esteem. There are men still wanting to be pampered and wanting their wife to baby them as if their wife were their mothers. That is not the role of a wife. Some men need to be men; the king in you would bring out the queen in her if men started respecting themselves. The same goes for women, you should not get married to replace your biological father or try to measure men up to your fathers standards. God has outlined in his word the criteria's for a man.

BEING HUNGRY OR
LOSING YOUR APPETITE

The Bible expresses to us in (NAS) **Mathew 5:6** that "blessed are those who hunger and thirst for righteousness, for they shall be satisfied." How is it that we are hungry to find out what the Bible says but are too afraid to read it? Why do we let those outside of the body of Christ dictate to Christians what God has for us? Nonbelievers say they don't believe, but they seem to know the Bible just as well as many Christians. There are individuals out there who seek to find faults in the Bible and who seek out and prey on weak Christians in order to make them doubt God or make them second guess what God has already revealed to them through his word. It is a mystery how one can be raised up on the Bible and all of its values and then later, seek another path to righteousness. How can we grow up with the word embedded in our hearts, being taught all our lives that God is real and that the Bible shows us a pathway to heaven, and then decide to take a detour later in life? Maybe this happens because we have lost the appetite for real food. Maybe we have gotten so satisfied with the junk food the world offers us that we have built up a tolerance for sweets.

How can we grow and be healthy if all we do is eat doughnuts, pies, cakes, candy, and all these sorts of sugary treats? We get so comfortable in eating these things that we don't realize the damage they are doing to our bodies until it's too late. That's the way the world presents itself to us. The world feeds us all this nonsense about how things should be and tell us things that are common sense in their eyes, even as they regularly change their views, thoughts, and opinions, while all along, God has a plan already set in place through his word, which he wants us to abide by. Although this plan has not changed and will not change, we seem to feel as if we know just as much as God does. Even though sweets are distracting and will eventually destroy our bodies if we continue to consume it, we should always know where to go for what is good and refuse to build up a tolerance for junk food that could particularly take us off of the track God has for us.

Sweets are appealing to the eyes and are dressed with all types of powdered sprinkles and appealing colors, but when we see broccoli, greens, squash, or beans that are good for our bodies, we often reject them right away. The vegetables will allow us to grow up healthy and strong in the future as we continue to live healthy life styles, but junk food will deteriorate our bodies as the years go on. The devil presents things to our flesh that allows us to enjoy them for the moment or for that current season, but he will never reveal the consequences to us while we are enjoying what he is putting fourth. We seem to know the name of God to call him when we get into jams or going through hard times, but as soon as we get to a place where we feel we don't need God, we seem to forget where he has brought us from.

If you say you believed in God before but now you've lost your appetite, maybe you weren't hungry enough or had truly not thirst after righteousness. Perhaps you were like a bandwagon fan of the Christian team, so when things were going your way, you were all excited. You cheered along with the other Christians, but when things weren't going in your favor or you had your doubts about something, you jumped ship and started cheering for another team. You may not even have known any of the players and what they stood for, and perhaps you didn't know their stats. As a true fan of God, you will know his starting lineup, and you will know his stats and what he has done in your heart. You will have all the signed memorabilia engraved into your heart, and you will want to be at every event that he will be attending, despite the cost of the tickets. Your true love will show that you are a true fan. Real fans defend their favorite teams or favorite players, no matter what happens. As a Christian, you often see other Christians excited about the Goodness of God, wanting to share it with their friends all the time. This is no different from sharing baseball, basketball, or football cards, and stats.

ASSUMING TO KNOW
JUST AS MUCH

E very person wants to tell the instructor or teacher how to instruct, when in fact, those individual joined a particular class just to learn. People want to tell the trainer how to train others, and they feel as if their methods of training will work. The real truth is that the trainer has already been trained to show the people what it is that they need to know. Who can tell you how to make a million dollars? Obviously, someone who has made a million dollars. The issue with society is that everyone wants to tell someone else either how to get ahead or how to get rich quick without working hard for it in a legitimate way. How is it that someone asks how to make a million dollars, but when the millionaire explains it, everyone all of a sudden has so much to bring to the table when it comes to making money? Where did this attitude come from?

We are people who want to put on an image and act as though we are trouble free and don't need help. In actuality, we are in the worst pain and hurt and are suffering beyond measure. If we learned to ask for assistance, be upfront about our issues, and be open, we would not be in half of the situations that we encounter. Stop approaching situations with an answer before assessing your situations for what they truly are. Don't allow your mouth to start rambling without actually knowing what is being presented. Doing this will not only save you from appearing ignorant but, in many cases, will help prevent your reputation from being tarnished. The Bible tells us in (NIV) **James 1:19,** "My dear brothers and sisters, take note of this: Everyone should be quick to listen, slow to speak and slow to become angry," which means that we should be careful not to assume anything. We should take time to know the outcomes before we get angry due to having jumped to conclusions. Many are familiar with the old saying that we shouldn't allow our mouths to write a check that our butts can't cash, or the saying that if we can't take the heat, perhaps we may need to get out of the kitchen. We as Christians need to just encourage one another by our actions. We need not to be so aggressive because things are not going our way or because we are too pigheaded and stubborn to hear others out before making fools out of ourselves.

SERIOUSNESS OF
RESPECTING CHRISTIANS

Ever wondered why many people don't take Christian's seriously? We should be just as strong as and even closer knit than any group, brotherhood, or organization that exists, and people should respect the power that we possess. The problem is that the church is out of order. It's just the same as if you go to a soda machine and put money in, and nothing comes out. You would be angry to find out that after you were thirsty and had invested money in the machine, the machine was out of order. That would truly anger you. And that's no different from going to church and investing years and time and not getting anything out of it because the church was out of order. People around you should wonder what are you doing and where you worship, in order that they may seek whatever you have and be blessed also. We should live our lives in such a way that are pleasing unto God.

Many do not seem to understand that God has so much to offer and could do so much for them. For example;, what if you saw something in a store, and you knew you just had to have it, and you were fortunate enough to have a friend in the store who noticed how badly you wanted the item?. Two days later, your friend approached you with the gift and watched the excitement on your face as you received it. The friend handed you the gift, and you in turn replied, with a thank you and were very appreciative of it. Your friend then replied, "You're welcome," to show you that he or she was glad you liked it. Well, that's no different from God wanting to have the final welcome for the gift he wants to present to you. Receiving a gift from a divine friend is no different from how we play out things on earth. God has a gift, who is Jesus. He wants to offer the gift to you because he has seen how excited you can get when you receive worldly gifts. God's gift is Jesus, and he has eternal life for you. God is offering it, but it's your choice to accept and be grateful and to share your gift with others. He truly wants to have the last word, just so he can tell you, you're welcome," and enjoy you enjoying your gift of eternal life.

BEING APPRECIATED

Ever wonder why the people you invest so much time in and mentor do not appreciate the sacrifices that you've made for them? You feel as if they are ungrateful, but later, they turn right around, looking for another favor, as if they didn't remember not displaying any gratitude for the last favor. Well, that's similar to how God looks at all these short comings and flaws that we have. He is gracious and merciful to forgive us over and over again. What gives us the right to go out and do things blatantly out of the will of God and then turn around and say sorry later?

It's truly breath taking to know that you genuinely care for an individual, and that person discredits all that you've done and just about everything you potentially stand for. Having an individually show you a lack of thanks behind your back is bad enough, but having someone say to your face, "You don't look out for my best interests" could potentially be a gut-wrenching blow to the body. That comes especially after you've invested so much. Many individuals truly do not understand the difference between being thankful and appreciative. Being thankful could be a mere sign of acknowledgement of a good deed that has been done. Being appreciative is that display of gratitude and the assurance to whomever expressing that you won't forget either the favor or the deed by your action from what was displayed. That's how God feels when he wants to give us help or even forgive us, for that matter, and we give God the run-around and still can't seem to do right by him. He feels that we are just thankful because things are good and we are happy for that moment. Thank God that he is not a human like us. He is able to handle the heart-breaks we cause. Taking on millions of prayers a day, he still provides for us, despite the number of times we may screw things up.

What if everyone had the mind of Christ, to make Christ like decisions? What if our thoughts were of heavenly things? We would have attitudes that could really change the ways people react or think. Don't be discouraged when you do something for people and they don't give you the proper thank you. Remember that whatever you do, God blesses those individuals in public for things done in private. And those who seek attention in public because they are so concerned about being seen will have already received their praise from the world. When you do things for attention or for people's approval, they do not last long. God knows that you're not real and that you are faking. He knows that you can fool some of the people on earth some of the time, but you won't be able to fool all of the people all of the time. This goes especially for believers. They truly feel that kindred spirits can feed off of each other's instincts or vibes.

Be content in what you have until God blesses you with more. When God blesses you, you should enjoy it with no setbacks. Often times, we bless ourselves and claim that it's from God. We later wonder why we can't make our car or house payments or why our possessions are being repossessed. God wants us to be prosperous, but he truly despises people's display of *greed*. Remember, what God has provided for you is for you and for your enjoyment. He won't bless you and curse you with the blessing at the same time!

CONSTANT
DISAPPOINTMENT

S ometimes people are sent to inform or to encourage us about what we should do about a particular issue in life. There are times when we know that we should be doing or saying something to stop someone from making a mistake that could potentially cost him or her heart-ache in the future. When the person refuses our assistance, we sometimes shun them and hope that what the person is doing fails, just so our point will be validated. Despite how sincere we might be, not everyone knows how to receive our wise words of wisdom.

There are times when you feel like Jeremiah, speaking until you're tired, especially when you're warning individuals about a wrong path or just informing them about issues. (Jeremiah was a prophet whose sole purpose was to reveal the sins of the people and the coming conse-quences, around 626 BC.) Indeed, the people may be headed down the wrong path, but sometimes it gets frustrating when they are not being attentive to you. You may get to a point where you feel like enough is enough, or at times you may just refuse to let them know the truth or give them any warnings. However, sometimes you're going to have to be persistent, despite what has happened in the past. You must remem-ber that yesterday is history, the future is a mystery, and living in the present is what's being required of you at that moment. You must also remember that you aren't the one who set yourself on this mission to inform people, God has you on assignment for his own reasons. Even when you're tired and don't feel like working one should remember that you're doing this mission for God. Despite how much you want to refuse, it's been given to you, so you have to obey, since we know that obedience is better than sacrifice. That was the same way Jeremiah felt when he didn't want to deliver God's message as God intended. He wanted to do it his way.

When God gives you that burning desire to do his will, despite other feelings, you need to do it. God can instill in you that burning desire to speak even when you don't want to. Have you ever had friends who brought their children over to your house? The children are jumping all over your furniture with their dirty or muddy shoes on. You wanted to say something to the children, but you refused to do so because you didn't want to upset the children's parents. And while this bad conduct was taking place, you were furious deep within and wanted to express to the children how angry you were about your furniture being ruined. That's no different than way Jeremiah felt speaking to a nation that re-fused to receive, listen, and obey. Have you ever done one thing be-cause of what you thought God wanted you to do but ended up doing something totally different and felt that God had tricked you into do-ing it, resulting in you blaming him for it? Having that mind-set is just ludicrous. We know that there may be differences between our expectations and God's because the Bible tells us in (NIV) **Isaiah 55:8–9,** "For My thoughts are not your thoughts, neither are your ways My ways" declares the Lord." 'As the heavens are higher than the earth, so are my ways higher than your ways and my thoughts than your thoughts." As much as we try to think on God's level, we can never do so. It will be beyond thinkable, and we will forever come up short.

THE PRIZE

Many individuals wonder what it will be like when the time comes for them to die. We know that there are many different ways to die, but there is only one true way to live, an eternal life. There is only one path-way to receiving what God has promised you. You wouldn't dare run an entire race looking back in hopes of winning the prize at the end, now would you? The prize always lies ahead of the runner at the end of the race. We should climb the stairway of life and do as Paul wrote in (KJV) **Philippians 3:14**. "I press toward the mark for the prize of the high calling of God in Christ Jesus." We are on a mission, and we should continue to press on until we receive the prize that God wants to give us if we obey and keep his word. Never stop climbing the steps of life to see what lies ahead.